121769 $1.50

S0-BLT-956

DATE DUE

MAY 2 8 1979			
MAY 2 4 19??			
DEC 0 7 1999			
GAYLORD 234			PRINTED IN U. S. A.

LIFE Pacific College
Alumni Library
1100 West Covina Blvd.
San Dimas, CA 91773

L.I.F.E. College Library
1100 Glendale Blvd.
Los Angeles, Calif. 90026

GETTING TO KNOW

GOD

PAUL
STEEVES

16161

231.07
St 32
c.1

InterVarsity Press
Downers Grove, Illinois 60515

L.I.F.E. College Library
1100 Glendale Blvd.
Los Angeles, Calif. 90026

© 1973
by Inter-Varsity Christian
Fellowship of the
United States of America.

All rights reserved.
No part of this book may
be reproduced in any
form without written
permission from
InterVarsity Press.

InterVarsity Press is the
book publishing
division of Inter-Varsity
Christian Fellowship.

ISBN 0-87784-357-0
Library of Congress Catalog
Card Number: 73-81574

Printed in the United
States of America

1,07
29

LIFE Pacific College
Alumni Library
1100 West Covina Blvd.
San Dimas, CA 91773

STUDY OUTLINE

*Those passages marked with an asterisk are the selections suggested for weekly group discussion.

Why Study the Nature of God?/ It is not oversimplification to say that one's thought and actions are shaped by his notions regarding the nature of God. "We tend by a secret law of the soul to move toward our mental image of God," Tozer said (*The Knowledge of the Holy*, New York: Harper, 1961, p. 9). C. S. Lewis once pointed out that the ancient Norsemen, whose chief god, Thor, was a god of war, were warlike people. The history of American Christianity affords a clear dual example of how notions about God influence thinking and actions. The liberal theology of about fifty years ago stressed the love and "Fatherhood" of God to the exclusion of other emphases and, consequently, gave rise to the "social gospel," an emphasis on doing good to all, thus bringing in the kingdom of God on earth through societal betterment. The basic gospel message concerning sin and personal salvation was largely ignored. On the other hand, in reaction to liberalism, fundamentalism often emphasized the severity and justice of God as a corrective to the sentimentality of liberalism's view. This emphasis frequently led, in practice, to a rigid legalism and minute distinctions concerning right and wrong—the essentials of Pharisaism—in fear of a severe God.

It appears, then, that one's view of God translates itself into a general predisposition for the conduct of his life. It should be clear that we cannot afford to have a distorted image of God if we desire to live and think in the way that he wills for us. Our idea of God must be as much in accord with what God is really like as is possible to us, weak and finite humans though we be.

And this is the reason that we can profit by careful, biblical study of the nature of God. What we *say* about God in our ordinary discourse about him may not correspond with what we really think about God. Our real notions concerning

God may be buried beneath our conventional prayers, conventional worship and conventional doctrines. To dig down to these real notions and to replace them with correct ones will require an intelligent and vigorous search and perhaps some painful self-examination. But our goal is too noble to miss.

What is more, many people's view of God is unworthy of their adult minds. They think of God in much the same way as they thought of him in their young, Sunday-school days. They have matured in many areas of their lives and thinking, but their view of God has remained infantile. "It is obviously impossible for an adult to worship the conception of God that exists in the mind of a child of Sunday-school age, unless he is prepared to deny his own experience of life," J. B. Phillips commented (*Your God Is Too Small,* London: Epworth, 1960, p. 7). Adults whose view of God has not "grown up" with them can either reject their belief in a god or isolate their belief in God from the rest of their experience. Neither rejection nor isolation accord with the biblical concept of a total life response to God. The antidote to this distortion is intensive study of God's own revelation of what he is like.

Thus, the aims of this series of studies are:
1/to see the true personality and character of God;
2/to bring our idea of God more into correspondence with what he is really like;
3/to stimulate our adult response to him on the basis of who he has shown himself to be.

Materials for This Study/ In addition to the study guide you will need:
1/a Bible/ preferably a modern-speech translation (most of the studies are based on Old Testament selections; the Scripture quotations in this guide are from the Revised Standard Version);
2/a pen/ recording discoveries as they are made in Bible study helps to shape and fix them in the mind. This extra step may seem to increase the study time, but it will prove its worth in the long run.

How to Use This Book/ This study guide has been designed to be used in groups. But it may also be used in regular personal Bible study.

For Personal Study/ Each daily study can be completed in about thirty minutes. First, read the suggested passage and try to discover its most important features. Then answer the questions. Third, read the comments. The comments are not intended to be an exposition of the study passage. The purpose of a study guide is to cause the student to interpret the passage himself. The comments are only a few observations about some aspect of the topic, designed to stimulate fuller comprehension. For this reason, the student should *consider the comments only a minor part of the study.* Finally, think through the application questions; this is the step of making the passage relevant to your life. Application of biblical truth includes two elements: one's personal response to God himself and one's overt actions in his daily life. Thus the application questions have been formulated to motivate you to think about your attitudes and relationship to God as well as about what he wants you to do.

With each study some suggestions are made for further investigation. If time permits or interest motivates you, follow these suggestions. Three books are mentioned frequently in the further study suggestions; they might be thought of as supplementary texts for this series:

The Living God by R. T. France (InterVarsity Press, 1970)
The Knowledge of the Holy by A. W. Tozer (New York: Harper and Row, 1961)
Knowing God by J. I. Packer (InterVarsity Press, 1973)

For Group Study/ This guide is designed for a pattern in which the group will meet weekly for five weeks to take up each of the five topics, and members of the group will study on their own the six daily studies, following the directions for personal study, in preparation for each group meeting.

For IVCF chapters and other large groups: A twenty-minute lecture followed by discussion in several small groups is probably the most profitable form of organization. The lecture should provoke thought about the topic as a stimulant to discussion. The discussion groups should concentrate on one of the daily studies. In the study outline (p. 5) an asterisk indicates the passage suggested as the focal point for discussion of each topic.

For campus or neighborhood Bible study groups: One of the daily studies is selected for study in the group. See the appendix for specific suggestions for the group meeting. Participants can share the discoveries they made in their personal study or raise questions which have occurred to them.

Some groups have found it better to use this guide in a different way. They have dispensed with the daily-weekly conception which underlies it and have used each "daily" study as the material for a weekly meeting. Used this way, this guide provides topics for up to thirty meetings of the group.

THE BEING OF GOD

"God is a Spirit, infinite, eternal and unchangeable in His being, wisdom, power, holiness, justice, goodness and truth." (Westminster Shorter Catechism)

This sentence is among the most profound ever framed by the human mind. It is just about the closest that human ability has come to defining God. Our study will attempt to expand our appreciation of the biblical truths which underlie this definition.

We embark on this study of the nature of God by taking note of three important qualifications:

1. *God is infinite/* Thus, God cannot be fully known. God is infinitely beyond our capacity to comprehend him because he is infinite. It therefore follows that we know only that about God which he has shown to us of himself. Thus, when we talk about God we can speak of things that are, indeed, true of him, but by no means can we speak exhaustively about him or about any truth about him.

2. *God is a unity/* For the purposes of study, we concentrate first on one aspect of God's declaration of who he is, and then on another aspect. For the purposes of study, we make an outline, separating these aspects. But God is not the sum of parts. God is one. All of God does everything that God does. All of God loves; all of God acts justly; God is "gracious in *all* his deeds" (Ps. 145:13). When we study one characteristic of God we must keep in mind that this characteristic is united to all the rest of God's nature. Thus we need not ever think of a supposed contradiction that may exist between different divine characteristics. Nor can we truly study one of his attributes in isolation from the rest. But we might appear to be doing so as we progress through this study. We can attempt to maintain a wholistic approach in our investigation by regularly relating the results of one study to those of the others.

3. *God is triune/* The doctrine of the Trinity expresses the conviction of Christians that the One God is a "God in Three Persons, Blessed Trinity." It might appear that this doctrine is ignored in this study—but we shall be studying characteristics which the Father, Son and Holy Spirit share because they are one God, and it will be well for us to remember that whatever we discover about God applies to each Person of the Trinity. As the Apostle Paul wrote, in Jesus Christ the whole fullness of deity dwells bodily (Col. 2:9).

study 1
the existence of god

Exodus 3
Questions
1/List what God says about himself. What does this chapter show about God?

2/List the variety of reactions that Moses has in this chapter. What does each show about Moses? Why does he react the way he does?

_____

_____

_____

_____

_____

_____

3/What plan does God outline for Moses?

_____

_____

Comments

There have been many men who have tried to discover a logical demonstration of the existence of God. This search for a proof of God has repeatedly proved to be futile. God is not known through logical demonstration. God is known to exist only when he shows that he exists by confronting individuals as he confronted Moses in this event. Moses knew God because God met him. We can have assurance of God's existence only when he meets us, in the person of Jesus Christ. Note, however (1) that there was an intriguing incident that attracted Moses' attention so that God could meet him, and (2) that Moses "turned aside" to meet God; that is, he was willing to investigate and discover whatever there was to discover.

Application

1/This chapter contains God's call to a man to perform a

work he assigned to him. As you review how Moses responded to this call, what can you learn about your response to God's call to you to do his will? How are you like Moses?

2/Moses was 80 years old at this time. He had spent 40 years as a member of the Pharaoh's family in Egypt; then he spent 40 years as a lowly shepherd. What does this show about preparation for God's service? What does this show about the kind of man God chooses? What does this mean for the experiences of your own life?

3/What does the fact that God waited 80 years before calling Moses show about how God may reveal his will? Are you too impatient to know God's will? Write down one specific need about which you will resolve to *wait*.

4/What does this study suggest about the way a person finds God? How can this help someone who is not a believer?

Further Study

Today's selection is the account of a principal event in the preparation for the Exodus ("going out") of the Hebrew nation from Egypt. The Exodus was the great day of the Hebrew nation—like the Fourth of July for the American nation. The Jews saw the nature of God clearly expressed in the Exodus (see Neh. 9:10—in the Exodus God "earned a name" with the Israelites). Throughout these studies reference will frequently be made to the Exodus. Become acquainted with the facts of this period of Jewish history:

1/Read the promise of the Exodus in Genesis 15:13-21.

2/Refer to question 3 above. Notice how God's plan corresponded to the events: Compare Exodus 3:18 with 4:29-31 and 5:1-3; 3:19 with 5:4; 3:20 with 6:1; 7:3-5; the plagues in chapters 7−10; 11:1; 12:31-33; 3:21-22 with 12:35-36.

3/Read quickly through chapters 13−18 of Exodus.

4/Read Psalms 78 and 105 to see how the Exodus was remembered centuries afterward. What place did it occupy in the history of Israel?

study 2
the name of god

Exodus 3
Questions
1/By what three designations does God identify himself?

_____

_____

_____

2/What does God say about his name (v. 15b)? What does
that mean?

_____

_____

3/Read Jeremiah 10:1-16. State in your own words the cen-
tral point of this section. What is the real difference between
the LORD and false gods?

_____

_____

_____

What is God called in this section?

_____

_____

_____

_____

_____

_____

_____

Comments

According to Hebrew custom, one's name was supposed to express one's character. So when Moses asked God to state his name he was asking for a means by which he could convey to his people what kind of God he represented. God answered the question "What is your name?" with the statement "I AM THAT I AM." Then he used "I AM" as the subject of a sentence, indicating that "I AM" equals "God."

The name by which God identified himself expressed three truths about his character. First, God is _self-existent_ (first person pronoun). All other things have an origin; they are created. But God is without origin; he is uncreated; he has life in himself, not from some outside source (see Jn. 5:26). And as such he is the origin of all else. Second, he is _eternal_. The name is a verb in the present, continuing tense. Third, he is _unique_. In making two parts of the declaration identical God identifies himself only in relationship to himself. No comparison can be made between him and another; there is no other god (see Deut. 6:4). God says simply "I AM THAT I AM."

Application

1/Compose a prayer of worship built around the truths about

God expressed in his name.

_____

_____

_____

_____

_____

_____

_____

2/The first three commandments of the Decalogue (Ex. 20:2-7) derive from the concepts implied by God's name. How do you obey them? In what ways might your actions be inconsistent with them?

_____

_____

_____

_____

_____

_____

3/If you want to know God's will, know God first.

Further Study
1/Read pages 11-17 in *The Living God.*

2/Read "The Self-Existence of God," chapter 5 in *The Knowledge of the Holy.*

3/Tozer says, "The natural man is a sinner because and only because he challenges God's selfhood in relation to his own" (*The Knowledge of the Holy,* p. 36). What does this mean? God is self-centered; but it is sinful in man to be so. Why?

4/See "God, Names of" in *The New Bible Dictionary* (IVP), pages 477-80. See "The Godhead" in *In Understanding Be Men* (IVP), pages 41-67, especially pages 50-51.

THE BEING OF GOD

study 3
the greatness of god

Isaiah 40
Questions
1/List the ways by which the prophet illustrates God's greatness.

_____

_____

_____

_____

_____

_____

_____

_____

_____

_____

2/Of what facts about the character and ways of God does Isaiah remind the Israelites (vv. 27-31)?

_____

_____

_____

_____

_____

Why are the Israelites mistaken about God (v. 27)?

_____

_____

What consolation does the prophet give (vv. 28-31 and 1-2)?

_____

_____

_____

Comments

Isaiah emphasizes God's greatness by comparison and contrast. God is shown to be greater than creation, supreme in wisdom, greater than nations, incompatible with idols, supreme over the rulers of the world, and the controller of the heavenly bodies.

The greatness of God is expressed in theological language by the term "transcendence." This word expresses the truth that God is not limited by space and time; he is above his creation; he is external to the world. The greatness of God must be reckoned with seriously.

But emphasis on this one fact to the exclusion of others leads to a gross distortion of the nature of God. In some people it has resulted in deism, which is the philosophical notion that God has no dealings with his world—that once he had made it, he left the universe to run on its own. In other people the truth about the transcendence of God has produced an almost paralyzing fear of God. In Scripture, the concept of transcendence is balanced by the concept of immanence (God's all-pervading presence in creation). God is near to help those who wait on him.

Application

1/Do you find it easy to take the greatness of God for granted and fail to give due respect? If the greatness of God impresses you today, spend a few minutes in silent reverence before him (v. 31).

2/Do you ever feel like the Israelites in verse 27? What answer does God give to you?

_____

_____

3/How can you avail yourself of God's strength when events seem to be against you (vv. 27-31)?

_____

_____

What does it mean to "wait on the Lord"?

_____

_____

L.I.F.E. College Library
1100 Glendale Blvd.
Los Angeles, Calif. 90026

Further Study

1/Notice how the concepts of transcendence and immanence are combined in Acts 17:24-28; Isaiah 57:15; 2 Chronicles 6:18-19.

2/See "The Divine Transcendence," chapter 13 in *The Knowledge of the Holy.*

3/How do Jesus and John the Baptist fulfill Isaiah 40:1-11?

4/One twentieth-century writer has said, "The old doctrine of transcendence is nothing more than an assertion of an outmoded view of the world." One frequently hears the claim that modern man cannot think of God as transcendent, as "up there" or "out there" beyond the earth. Do you think that these criticisms have any validity? In what ways are they a misrepresentation of the doctrine of transcendence?

study 4
"god is a spirit"

John 4:20-24
Deuteronomy 4:9-20

Questions

1/Why are images of God (idols) prohibited?

2/What misconception about God does the woman in John 4 have? How is her notion like that of a person who makes images?

3/Express in your own words the connection between God's nature and worship that is implied in Jesus' answer to the woman.

Comments

It is natural for humans to create images of God, some material, some mental. But images of God tend to debase God because he is not limitable to our images of him. An image insults his character.

Jesus' words "God is a Spirit" express two truths about God, one negative and one positive. God is *not* a corporeal being. Hence he is not confined to one place, which implies that worship of God need not be restricted to one location. Hence, also, images of God are forbidden. God *is* a personal being. This implies that God has self-consciousness and self-determination (he wills). A view of God as "impersonal force" is as insulting to his character as an idol.

Application
1/Examine your notion of God. In what ways is it limited? Are you idolatrous in your conception of God (that is, do you think him to be really like your mental image of him)?

2/How can the truth that "God is a Spirit" affect your prayers and your awareness of his presence today?

Further Study
1/Do you agree with the statement "God is a person"? Some Christians do not. They say that such a statement makes God like man. Can you suggest a better word than "person" for this description? Consult "God as a Person" in *The Living God*, pages 19-20.

2/Explain the following passages which seem to contradict the statement "God is a Spirit": Exodus 33:18-23 (cf. 33:22 and 34:5-8); Exodus 24:9-11; passages that speak of the "hand" (Ps. 75:8), "ear" (Is. 37:17), "arms" (Is. 52:10), "eyes" (2 Chron. 16:9), "wings" (Ps. 91:4) of God. How do you understand Genesis 1:26-27?

study 5
the knowledge of god

Psalm 139
Questions
1/List the things which the psalmist says God knows.

_____

_____

_____

_____

_____

_____

_____

_____

_____

2/Describe the various kinds of response to God's knowledge
that David displays.

_____

_____

_____

_____

_____

_____

_____

3/Why does the psalmist ask God to know his heart and thoughts? Why these rather than his actions?

_____

_____

4/To what extremes does God's knowledge extend (cf. Ps. 147:4-5; Mt. 10:29-31)?

_____

_____

Comments

God is infinite in knowledge. Sometimes this truth is expressed by saying that God is *omniscient*. There is nothing, past, present or future, that God does not know. He knows the end even at the beginning (Is. 46:9-10). He knows the whole of our lives (v. 16), our thoughts and actions six years ago and ten years from now. To emphasize the totality of God's knowledge Scripture points out that God knows details about enormous things (the majestic stars) and about tiny things (our hairs). It is no wonder that David responds with awe to the scope of God's knowledge.

Application

1/What does it mean for you that God knows so much about

your thoughts?

That he knows about all the days of your life?

2/Read 1 Chronicles 28:9 and see how David applied the truth of Psalm 139 in his advice to his son. How will you follow this advice?

3/Can you pray the psalmist's prayer of verses 23 and 24?

Further Study

1/In the language of Scripture, to say that someone "knows" means more than simply that he is aware of certain facts. Enlarge your understanding of the implications of the statement "Thou knowest me right well" by studying the following uses of the verb "to know": Amos 3:2; Genesis 4:1; Hosea 13:4-5; Romans 8:28-30.

2/If God knows everything, why should we pray? See Matthew 6:8-13. What teaching about prayer and God's knowledge is suggested in 2 Chronicles 6:29-31?

3/On the basis that God knows everything, some philosophers have said that man does not have free will; others, emphasizing that some actions are freely chosen by man, have said that God is not omniscient (because if decisions are really free, then even God cannot know what decision a man will make until he makes it). What do you think of this dilemma? See *In Understanding Be Men*, page 46.

4/See "The Divine Omniscience," chapter 10 in *The Knowledge of the Holy*.

Psalm 139:7-24

Questions

1/Where must one go to escape God?

At what places does David say he will find God?

2/What would be the implications—for theology, for your life—if one could escape from God?

3/What kind of presence is it that God has (v. 7)? What does this mean?

Comments

God is infinite in presence. Sometimes this truth is expressed by saying that God is *omnipresent*. He is present everywhere, in a spiritual sense. "He is not far from each one of us," Paul said (Acts 17:27). Since he is close by us, we can have confidence that if we seek him we shall find him.

Another way to speak of this characteristic of God is to say that we are always in God's presence. "Can a man hide himself in secret places so that I cannot see him? says the Lord. Do I not fill heaven and earth?" (Jer. 23:24) We can then think of prayer as simply beginning to speak to someone in whose presence we already are. Thus we can "pray always" as Paul directs. To "practice the presence of God" means always to recognize that God is everywhere present with us, even when we do not particularly feel it.

Application

1/In what ways do you sometimes act as if it were possible to get away from God (for example, when you sin; when you fail to trust him; when you forget him; when you do well)? List specific examples.

_____

_____

_____

_____

2/Do you ever wish that God were not omnipresent? Why?

_____

_____

3/How can you live today with special awareness of God's presence?

_____

_____

Further Study

1/How is pantheism ("everything is God") a perversion of the doctrine of omnipresence? How does study 3 correct pantheism?

2/Brother Lawrence learned to be acutely aware in all his life of God's presence with him. His experiences are preserved for us in the little booklet, *The Practice of the Presence of God.*

3/See "God's Omnipresence," chapter 14 in *The Knowledge of the Holy.*

topic b
THE SOVEREIGNTY OF GOD

The "sovereignty of God" is the phrase by which we express the truths that God is supreme; he is King; he is almighty. The meaning of this phrase is expressed in the words of Scripture: "Thine, O Lord, is the greatness, and the power, and the glory, and the victory, and the majesty; for all that is in the heavens and in the earth is thine; thine is the kingdom, O Lord, and thou art exalted as head above all" (1 Chron. 29:11); "For dominion belongs to the Lord, and he rules over the nations" (Ps. 22:28). No Christian disputes the sovereignty of God. But he may live so as to contradict the rule of God over him. Or he may not understand the meaning of the sovereignty of God. Only a true understanding, in thought and in practice, of God's sovereignty opens the door to correct biblical understanding, true worship and successful Christian living. This week we shall study some of the aspects of a truly challenging and immense subject: the sovereignty of God.

study 1
god's creation

Psalm 104

Questions

1/How does the psalmist describe the origin of the natural world?

_____

_____

_____

_____

_____

2/What specific provisions does God make for his creatures?

_____

_____

_____

3/In what places does the writer find purpose in nature? How does he account for this pattern of purpose?

_____

_____

_____

_____

4/How does the writer describe God's continuing relationship to his creation?

_____

_____

Comments
The sovereignty of God derives from the fact of creation. God made all things and therefore he has the right of governing them. He has the prerogative of determining their purposes, because he made them. One of the beauties of God's creation is the inter-relatedness of the elements within the creation (for example, grass grows for cattle to eat, v. 14; trees grow for the birds to build their nests in, v. 17). With the increased knowledge of nature that we have now, we should be able to say with even more meaning, "O Lord, how manifold are thy works."

A second great truth that the psalmist emphasizes is that God not only made the universe, but he continues to keep it going (especially vv. 27-30). God is both the Creator and the Sustainer of the world. As the psalmist saw things, even the lions stalking their food in the wild are actually seeking nourishment from God's hand. God is so intimately involved with his creation that Jesus could say that the death of a small sparrow can occur only by the will of God (Mt. 10:29).

Application
1/What are David's responses to his study of God's creation?

Respond today in the same way David did.

2/Does your study of the creation (which includes man, of course) lead you to praise God? Think about how the classes you are taking in school or the reading you do on your own can move you to respond to God.

Further Study

1/See "God the Creator" in *In Understanding Be Men,* pages 57-62, and "God's Providence and Divine Government," pages 62-65.

2/Note how the New Testament says specifically of Jesus Christ what this psalm says of God: Colossians 1:16-17; Hebrews 1:2-3; John 1:1-4.

3/Read "The Almighty Creator" and "The Providence of God" in *The Living God,* pages 71-73 and 81-85.

4/Job 38—41 develops thoughts similar to those of today's study. How could you use the teaching of these passages to develop a biblical perspective on issues raised by the "Ecological Movement"?

study 2
god's purpose

Isaiah 43:1-7
Ephesians 1:3-14

Questions

1/To what fact does Isaiah call the attention of the readers in verse 1? What reason does he give for God's having created man (v. 7)?

2/How is God's concern for the people of Israel shown in this section?

3/In Ephesians, Paul is writing about God's purpose in blessing us in Christ with "every spiritual blessing" (that is, providing salvation for us). List all the things that Paul explicitly declares God did (or does) in his plan for salvation in all its aspects. (Look for verbs in the active voice.)

_____

_____

_____

_____

_____

4/What was God's purpose in providing salvation? (Paul mentions it three times; compare Is. 43:21.)

_____

5/The word "glory" occurs several times in these sections. What do you understand to be the meaning of "glory"? What is God's glory?

_____

_____

_____

Comments

God's sovereignty is exercised in his determining the purpose of his creation. In answer to the question "Why did God create?" we must say "He did it for his own glory." God's creating was a self-directed, self-expressive, self-satisfying act. Just as a painter "creates" a masterpiece to express himself, God created to express himself and to declare what he is. God's glory is that which makes God God. His glory is his exclusive prerogative. We understand this from his declaration: "For my own sake, for my own sake, I do it, for how should my name be profaned? My glory I will not give to another" (Is. 48:11; cf. Is. 42:8). The universe, in the intention God had for it, is God-directed and God-centered. The essence of sin is to become directed toward something other than God (usually it is one's self). C. S. Lewis describes the key element in the fall of man (Gen. 3) as "the movement whereby a creature (that is, an essentially dependent being whose principle of existence lies not in itself but in another) tries to set up on its own, to exist for itself" (*The Problem of Pain*, London: Fontana, 1957, p. 63). In our own experiences we repeat and perpetuate this movement away from God. But, as a thing is only good when it is fulfilling its intended function, so we can only be good when we are centered about God's glory in our thoughts and actions.

Application
1/What motivates your life—God's glory or something else?

2/Do you really believe that God's words in Isaiah 43:1-2, 4 apply to you?

3/How can your life be more directed toward God, more God-centered?

4/If the primary reason God saved you was for the praise of his own glory, how should you think about your salvation?

How can you conduct yourself accordingly?

Further Study

1/In his science fiction work *Perelandra,* C. S. Lewis amplifies the tension between the creature's independence and proper dependence.

2/Supplementary study: The concept of the glory of God is very profound, and careful study of it can be rewarding. The following topical study takes longer than most of the other suggestions for further study given in this guide. Perhaps you will want to devote a separate day's study time to it.

A/ What does the word "glory" mean in the Old Testament when not referring to God?

Psalm 49:16-17   for what is "glory" a synonym?

Psalm 30:12   where the RSV puts "soul" the original Hebrew word is the word for "glory"; compare the King James Version here. See also Psalms 16:9 and 57:8, where the same words appear. If "glory" and "soul" are synonymous, what does "glory" mean?

Isaiah 60:13   what words are used here to specify and expand "glory"?

Micah 1:15   to what does "glory" refer here in the context of predicted conquest?

Proverbs 25:2   "glory" here refers to activities. What does this imply?

B/ What are the characteristics of the "glory of God"?

Exodus 24:17   what was the glory of God like?

Ezekiel 1:26-28   verse 28 states that what is described here is "the likeness of the glory of the Lord." What was it like?

2 Chronicles 5:13-14; 7:1-3   how is the "glory" manifested here?

Ezekiel 10:3-5, 18-19; 11:22-23   what things are implied about the glory of the Lord by Ezekiel's report of what he witnessed (cf. Ex. 40:34-38)?

Numbers 14:1-24   what is implied by the fact that the "glory of the Lord" moves about, can be seen, and is associated with special communications from God to man?

C/ What is "God's glory"?

Exodus 33:18-23   when Moses asks God to show him his glory, what does God say Moses can and cannot see?

Isaiah 11:9; Habakkuk 2:14   what is the relationship between the "glory of the Lord" and "the Lord"?

Psalm 106:19-20   how does the parallel construction here point out what "glory" means?

Jeremiah 2:10   for whom is "glory" synonymous here?

D/ What is the relationship between God's glory and his creation?

Psalm 19:1-4   how does nature declare God's glory?

Psalm 29:1-2   how should man respond to God's glory?

Psalm 96:3   how can men declare God's glory?

Summarize in several sentences your conclusions about the meaning of the concept of the glory of God. Refer to "The Glory of God" in *The Living God,* pages 66-68.

study 3
god's supremacy

Psalm 47
Psalm 93
Questions
1/In these two psalms, how does the psalmist describe God's supremacy?
Why is he rightfully supreme?

Over whom and what?

For how long?

2/In what ways is God's kingship emphasized?

Comments

"The Lord reigns": To say that the Lord is King is to say that God is sovereign. It is to say that he is on the throne of the universe. Jehoshaphat recognized the sovereignty of God when he said, "O Lord, God of our fathers, art thou not God in heaven? Dost thou not rule over all the kingdoms of the nations? In thy hand are power and might, so that none is able to withstand thee" (2 Chron. 20:6).

The 93rd psalm was probably written to celebrate the return of the Jewish people from many years of captivity in the foreign land of Babylon. Great ill had befallen the Jews (expressed in Ps. 137), and their response had been both doubt that God still cared for them and faith that God would again show his favor toward them.

Then the time came when the Jews returned to their native land and in this deliverance, as in the Exodus, the Jews saw the evidence that their God was the Great God, the King over all kings. Notice in this psalm the allusions to kingship: As all kings, God has robes, a throne, enemies over which he triumphs; he issues sovereign decrees; he has a special dwelling place.

Application

1/How can God really be a king to you?

_____

_____

_____

2/What does the psalmist say are the appropriate responses to the supreme God?

_____

_____

Worship God for his supremacy.

Further Study

1/In the light of today's study, examine Daniel 2:20-22; 4:24-26; Revelation 1:5.

2/Tozer says: "God's sovereignty is the attribute by which He rules His entire creation, and to be sovereign God must be all-knowing, all-powerful and absolutely free" (*The Knowledge of the Holy*, p. 115). Why, do you think, is this so? See "The Sovereignty of God," chapter 22 in *The Knowledge of the Holy*.

3/The fourth chapter of the Revelation is a representation of the kingship of God in a vision of his throne room. This chapter may serve as a basis for study or for worship of God's supremacy.

study 4
human response

1 Chronicles 29:10-22

Questions

1/Why are verses 10-13 in this offertory prayer? What is said about God?

2/What is the difference between saying "Thine is the greatness and the power . . ." and "Thou are great, powerful, glorious . . ."?

3/What does David say about himself and the people for whom he is praying?

What is a proper response to God's greatness?

Comments

The sovereignty of God is expressed in practice in the acknowledgement that all things rightfully belong to him and we are but strangers (v. 15), not owners; that is, we are in temporary possession of the world and our material things. Thus, we thank God for our food before eating. Thus, too, we willingly contribute of our material substance to God's work.

But because we are selfish we are not naturally inclined to give willingly to God. It is a product of God's work in us that we are able to do God's work. Hence, we cannot see our giving (or any work we do for God) as some kind of favor we do for him but only as the work he does through us (cf. Phil. 2:13: God works in us so that we will *want* to do his will as well as do it). There can be no place for pride in this, can there?

Application

1/What do you learn in today's study about the giving of money to God's work?

2/What attitudes and actions can people have which are inconsistent with this teaching? Are any of these yours?

3/How is the giving of money a proper response to God's sovereignty?

What else is properly given in response to God's sovereignty?

Think of a way in which you can worship in deed as well as in word this week.

Further Study

1/Find the principles of giving taught in 2 Corinthians 8 and 9.

2/See the studies in "Possessions," unit 11 in *Grow Your Christian Life* (IVP).

3/Work through the studies on giving in *Enrich Your Life* (IVP).

Historical note: The setting for this prayer and exhortation by David is the end of David's forty-year reign as king of Israel. Solomon is his choice as successor, and the assembling of the people in today's study is for the purpose of handing on the succession to him. In the first nine verses of the chapter David disclosed to the assembly that he had been preoccupied in his life with the building of a magnificent temple for God, but that God had prevented him from actually building it. So, David had assembled the funds and materials for construction and bequeathed them to Solomon. Following David's example the noblemen had made a huge offering to God, and the prayer is the offertory prayer that David made to dedicate these offerings to God.

study 5
god in history

Isaiah 8:1-8
Isaiah 10:5-15

Questions

1/What does Isaiah predict (8:4-8)? Why will these events occur? (Compare v. 6 with Is. 1:18-20; see Is. 5:18-26.)

2/How are the king of Assyria and his role in God's plan described? What does this show about how God fulfills his plans?

3/Why does Isaiah call the Assyrians' work of war and destruction the Lord's work (10:12)?

4/How does the king of Assyria view his role (10:7-11, 13-14)?

Why will God punish him eventually (10:12-15)? (See also 2 Kings 19:20-28.)

Comments

The sovereignty of God is expressed in his ruling in the affairs of men (Dan. 4:25). In order to accomplish all of his purpose, God uses any people who will contribute to the working of his will, whether they are conscious of it or not. Isaiah had an acute recognition that history is the outworking of God's will in his gracious and just dealings with man. The believer knows that history is not a meaningless succession of events, even though he may not understand what God's purpose is in the disturbing and chaotic conditions that develop in human affairs. Isaiah knew what God was doing in his time because God revealed it to him. The function of a prophet was to declare the purpose of God in particular events. In God's declaring his purpose we learn the truth that he is in control of history (cf. Dan. 2:19-23).

Application

1/If God is active in history, how should you react to the uncertainty of international conditions?

2/If God acts in history, what course should your own planning take (cf. Jas. 4:12-15)?

3/If God used an ungodly king to get his job done, what does this suggest about the attitude you should have toward God's using you?

Further Study

1/See "The Sovereignty of God" in *The Living God,* pages 74-79.

2/Isaiah 45 reflects an understanding of pagan nations and history similar to that of this study. In Isaiah 45 the king is the Persian King Cyrus. Study Isaiah 45 to see more of God's use of men who do not recognize him.

3/What attitude should we have toward governments and authorities in the light of today's study (see Rom. 13:1-7; 1 Tim. 2:1-4; 1 Pet. 2:13-17)? How should we view the role of the Christian in politics? How should we pray for authorities?

4/What does Romans 9:14-23 contribute to the understanding of God in history? Historical note: At the time when Isaiah wrote (740 B.C.) Assyria, located to the north and east of Israel, was emerging to military greatness and beginning a program of imperialist expansion. Damascus (Is. 8:4) was the capital of the declining power, Syria.

study 6
god's sovereign choice

1 Chronicles 17
Questions
1/Of what does the Lord remind David (vv. 7-8)?

_____

_____

2/What promises does God make to David (vv. 8-14)?

_____

_____

_____

_____

_____

_____

3/Characterize David's response to what the Lord says to him
(vv. 16-27).

_____

4/What does David say about God?

_____

_____

_____

_____

_____

About Israel?

_____

_____

_____

_____

About God's relation to Israel?

_____

_____

_____

_____

5/What was God's purpose in choosing to deal with David

LIFE College Library
1100 Glendale Blvd.
Los Angeles, Calif. 90026

and with Israel in the way he did (vv. 21-24)?

Comments

In this study, again, we see God active in history to accomplish his sovereign purpose. God selected David to be the forefather of his Messiah (vv. 12-14); God selected the people of Israel to be the nation of his Christ. God made the moves in this selecting (v. 21: "... God went ...") for his own purposes and without discernible reason. Moses discussed this selection that God made in Deuteronomy 7:6-11, where he pointed out that there was no good reason for God's selecting Israel instead of any other people except that God chose to love them. And to what end did he do this? It was so that he could be their God (v. 24). God chooses us as his people not to save us only but to *be a God to us*: to be the one source of all our joy, the one object of all our love, and the one end of our very being. God becomes involved with his own people.

Application

1/Are you letting God really be a God to you in all your life, or are you just receiving your salvation from him passively? What do you need to do in order that God can more truly be God to you? (Perhaps Jer. 11:1-5 will suggest some answers.)

2/How can you use David's prayer as an example for you to follow?

3/What new insights into the nature of God have you gained in studying his sovereignty? How can they affect your life this week?

_____

_____

_____

4/Worship God for his sovereignty.

Further Study
1/The selection of Israel began in Genesis with the selection of Abraham. Study especially Genesis 12:1-3 and 15:1-21.
2/See "Divine Sovereignty and Human Responsibility," chapter 2 in *Evangelism and the Sovereignty of God* by J. I. Packer (IVP).

THE HOLINESS OF GOD

Our series of studies is divided into two major units. Topics A and B have covered those qualities which are God's, in himself, sometimes called *absolute* attributes. Topics C, D and E will consider those qualities in God which imply and produce moral action on his part, called *moral* attributes. Of course, such division can be misleading, though it is convenient, since as we have already emphasized God is a Unity.

In the Westminster definition (see page 11) God's moral attributes are subsumed under the items ". . . infinite, eternal and unchangeable . . . in His *holiness, justice, goodness and truth.*" The apostle John succinctly expresses the moral attributes of God's nature in two definitive phrases: "God is light" (1 Jn. 1:5) and "God is love" (1 Jn. 4:8). The former statement expresses the holiness of God, the latter the goodness of God. The next three topics explore these exciting themes in God's revelation of his nature.

Sometimes in theology God's moral attributes are called his *communicable* attributes as over against his *incommunicable* (absolute) attributes. "Communicable" draws attention to the truth that these divine characteristics can and should be practiced by men in imitation of God. Thus one application of each of the following studies entails the question of how we can reflect in our lives the quality of God emphasized in the study.

study 1
"holy, holy, holy"

Isaiah 6:1-8
Questions
1/By what three phrases does Isaiah describe his vision of the Lord in verse 1? What do these phrases express about God?

_____

_____

_____

2/When heavenly beings praise God, what word do they choose to express his character? (See Rev. 4:8-11.) What might be the reason that they say this word three times?

_____

3/From the following verses, construct your definition of _holy_: Exodus 20:8; Isaiah 57:15; Hosea 11:9; Habakkuk 1:12-13; Leviticus 11:44-45; 1 Timothy 6:15-16.

_____

_____

_____

4/Note the effects of the vision of the Lord on both the temple and Isaiah. What do these effects show about the meaning of God's holiness?

Comments

Many times in Scripture God is called the Holy One (Ps. 89:18; Is. 43:3, 14-15; Is. 47:4) because no other word expresses the nature of God as well as "holy" does. Two principal concepts are contained in the idea of God's holiness. They are juxtaposed in some of the verses cited in question 3. (1) God's holiness is his separateness (his otherness or distinctness) from man and the rest of his creation. It is what he is as God, his glory: "Who is like thee, O Lord . . . Who is like thee, majestic in holiness . . .?" (Ex. 15:11). (2) God's holiness is his moral perfection—light in contrast to darkness (1 Jn. 1:5). Notice that in 1 Timothy 6:16 Paul says it is the light in which God dwells that makes God separate.

The origins of the Hebrew word translated "holy" reflect both concepts. The root word referred originally to the action of *cutting,* whence it came to signify a *separation* or *setting apart,* then took on the ideas of *purity* and *brightness.* In selecting this word to express what he is like, God declared the complexity of the very essence of his nature.

God's holiness is an utterly transcendent quality, which is inadequately conceived if we think of its meaning merely that God is sinless (a negative condition). This absolute, positive transcendence gives rise to the three-fold ascription "Holy, Holy, Holy"; there is just no other way to express what God is like.

Application

1/How is Isaiah's response to God's holiness an appropriate example to follow?

2/What great comfort is contained in verses 6 and 7 for the person who trembles before God's holiness ("woe is me")?

_____

_____

3/When Jesus taught his disciples to pray he placed a recognition of God's holiness at the head of the prayer (Mt. 6:9, "hallowed" means "made holy"). Awareness of God's holiness should lead us not to cringing fear but to heartfelt praise (see Ps. 22:3). How can you respond in this way?

_____

_____

4/What practical results should an awareness of God's holiness have in your life (1 Pet. 1:15-16)? List some specific steps you can take.

_____

_____

_____

_____

Further Study
Look through a hymnal and copy some verses about God's holiness which can help you in your personal praise of him.

study 2
the law of god

Exodus 19:7—20:21
Questions
1/Read quickly through the entire passage. Describe in a few phrases the scene here portrayed.

_____

_____

_____

_____

_____

2/Why was this event so elaborate and dramatic, with smoke, thunder, lightning, precautions, etc.? God did not always appear in so impressive a manner (e.g., when he met Moses, Ex. 3, or when he met Elijah, 1 Kings 19:11-12).

_____

_____

_____

3/How did the people respond to the scene?

Comments
God's holiness is the source of moral standards for men. In his law, God expressed in a tangible way the meaning of his attribute of holiness. God first demonstrated his awesome holiness to the Israelites by the enacted parable of the transformation of Mount Sinai, so that they would take him seriously and not break his law (Ex. 20:20). The commandments which God then gave declare the requirements of holiness in human life. The Ten Commandments are not meaningless or arbitrary laws established by a harsh god. They are the expression of the perfectly holy character of God from which his will derives. They are statements of how the holiness of God is properly translated into human society through human actions.

In the first four commandments (20:2-11) God decrees the manner in which men are to acknowledge and respect his uniqueness (i.e., his holiness). In the remaining injunctions he sets the conditions by which holiness of life is to be expressed. All the commandments were summarized by Jesus in two statements: Love God; love man (Mt. 22:35-40). God's law expresses what infinite holiness and love demand.

Application
1/How seriously do you take God's law?

2/Your attitude concerning God's law reveals much about your real attitude toward his holiness. How would you describe your response to God's holiness? Are you awed by God's holiness?

L.I.F.E. College Library
1100 Glendale Blvd.
Los Angeles, Calif. 90026

3/Think through each of the Ten Commandments and try to discover how you can more perfectly respect God's holiness by fulfilling them. List some action you can take in obedience to each commandment. Be personal and specific.

Further Study

Ten Great Freedoms by Ernst Lange (IVP) develops the meaning of the Ten Commandments. See also *Basic Christianity* by John R. W. Stott (IVP), pages 64-70, and *Unsplitting Your Christian Life* by Michael Griffiths (IVP), chapters 4–9.

study 3
the justice of god

Psalm 99

Questions

1/List all the images by which the psalmist expresses and emphasizes God's holiness.

_____

_____

_____

_____

What reactions to it does he urge?

_____

_____

_____

2/What specific actions on God's part proceed from his holiness (vv. 4, 8)?

_____

_____

3/What part does God's law play in this psalm?

4/What connections are drawn here among holiness, law and justice?

Comments

In order to appreciate fully what Scripture teaches about God's justice, one must be aware of a quirk in most English translations of the Bible. In English there are two words, "justice" and "righteousness," which represent in almost every instance only one Hebrew and one Greek word in the original text of Scripture. Thus, in Scripture "justice" and "righteousness" are absolutely identical. Wherever the word "righteousness" occurs it would be appropriate to read "justice."

Justice is the holiness of God in action. Justice means the application of law. If the law of God derives from his holiness, as we saw in the previous study, then God's justice similarly is the practical demonstration of his holiness. The prophet expressed this truth clearly: "The Holy God shows himself holy in righteousness" (Is. 5:16). Justice is God's treatment of his creatures in a manner consistent with his holy nature. Or, as Tozer says, "When God acts justly He is ... simply acting like Himself" (*The Knowledge of the Holy*, pp. 93-94). God's justice further expresses itself in his requiring people to be just, that is, to keep his law. Hence, as our psalm points out, God revealed that law to his people, aided them in their keeping of it, punished them when they failed to keep it, forgave when they repented.

Application
Identify all the clauses of this psalm that are in the imperative mood (direct or indirect commands). How can you heed these in worship, in thought, in action?

_____

_____

_____

_____

_____

Further Study
1/Read "The Righteousness of God" in *The Living God,* pages 92-96.
2/See "The Justice of God," chapter 17 in *The Knowledge of the Holy.* Reflect on the following intriguing question: Does God do a thing because it is just, or is a thing just because God does it? What are the implications of the alternative answers implied in this question?

study 4
god's justice applied

Micah 6

Questions

1/In what spirit and for what purpose, do you think, is the question of verse 6 asked?

2/What possible answers enter the questioner's mind?

What do they show about the questioner?

3/What are the three requirements presented to the questioner in reply? What does each mean?

4/Describe the contrast between the questioner's contemplated approach to God and God's requirements.

_____

_____

How is a similar idea shown in Amos 5:21-24?

_____

_____

5/Of what sins is Israel guilty (vv. 9-16)?

_____

_____

_____

_____

_____

_____

What will be the consequences?

_____

_____

_____

_____

_____

_____

Comments

What should a person do when he becomes aware of God's holiness and justice? The human mind senses a need for some appropriate response to the "God on high" (v. 6), that is, the Holy God. The questioner in this section is conscious of this need because he knows his guilt before God. But he mistakes religious ceremony for the proper response to God. The human mind searches for a ritual to perform which will win approval in God's sight, and through the ages man has devised all manner of formalities and activities, both external works and emotional states, to satisfy the demands of God's holiness. But the response God requires is a practical reflection of his holy character in a life of justice, kindness and humility before him.

Justice and kindness can be practiced only in relationship to other people. They express the social, or manward, aspect of the life God requires. A humble walk with God is the true piety with which God is pleased. Repeatedly Scripture points to our twofold responsibility before God: love for God and love for others. Both the manward and Godward dimensions must be present for one to "come before the Lord." The apostle James expressed the same idea: "Religion that is pure and undefiled before God and the Father is this, to visit the orphans and widows in their affliction [*justice and kindness*] and to keep oneself untainted from the world [walk with God]" (Jas. 1:27).

Application

1/Is your practical response to God's holiness and justice the kind which he requires? By what actions specifically are you doing justice and loving kindness in your life?

_____

_____

_____

How are you walking humbly with your God?

_____

_____

_____

2/Consider what part the following might have in your practical response: involvement in political or social action, obeying regulations and laws, witnessing, attending church or prayer and Bible study groups, contributing money to organizations or fund drives. Write down some specific steps you can take.

_____

_____

_____

study 5
the justice of god in the salvation of men

Romans 3:19-31

Questions

1/What functions does the law serve in the judgment of God (vv. 19-21)?

2/In what ways does God's provision of salvation through the death of Christ prove "that he himself is righteous" or just (v. 26)?

3/How is one made righteous (just or justified) before God?

4/How does the concept of justification by faith "uphold the law" (v. 31)?

Comments

Paul said in Romans 1 that he was not ashamed of the gospel because through the gospel God's justice is shown. That thought is here in chapter 3, too. This concept is amazing. We should expect him to say, "Because God is just, he condemns the sinner." But he does not. He says, in effect, "Because God is just, he accepts the sinner as also being just." Here is the beauty, the preciousness, of the gospel. No wonder Paul said he was not ashamed of it.

But how can God act this way? He can because he accepts the obedient life and death of Jesus Christ (Rom. 5:19) as adequate to atone (pay) for the sins of men. We must not presume to be able to understand how this works. We must only realize that this is what Jesus has shown us about God—that he is willing to accept us. We have every good reason in the light of this week's study to fear God and cower before him. But Jesus tells us that this is not necessary. And this is what it is to be "justified by faith." It is to believe with all our heart that what Jesus told us about God is so—God accepts those who love the Lord Jesus. "If a man loves me, he will keep my word, and my Father will love him, and we will come to him and make our home with him" (Jn. 14:23).

Application

1/Are you rejoicing in your acceptance by the great God?

2/What should be your attitude to the law of God if you are a believer in Jesus Christ?

Further Study

1/See "The Holiness of God," chapter 21 in *The Knowledge of the Holy*.
2/Consider which is the fundamental attribute of God, his holiness or his love. Although there is no contradiction between these attributes, the determination of

which is considered in Scripture as more fundamental would be useful for our analytical minds and our ethics, since we inevitably think of them separately and emphasize one or the other. God's infinite unity, to be sure, makes such priority unnecessary. It is popular today to consider God's love as more fundamental and to consider the other moral attributes as issuing therefrom. However, it would appear that Scripture treats God's holiness as the more fundamental attribute: (1) the eternal praise of God is that he is holy (Rev. 4:8); (2) God's relations with man are determined by his holiness in that (a) no man can see God without holiness (Heb. 12:14) and (b) redemption was a vindication of God's holiness; (3) God's name is given as "holy" but never as "love" (Is. 57:15). If holiness is the attribute which is logically prior to all others, how is your understanding of God affected? How are your ethics affected?

study 6
the judgment of god

Psalm 96
Nahum 1:2-8

Questions

1/What facts about the Lord does the psalmist emphasize?

_____

_____

_____

_____

_____

_____

_____

_____

_____

_____

_____

_____

Why is the Lord rightfully the judge?

2/For what attitudes does the psalmist call in response to the Lord as the coming judge (Ps. 96:10-13)? Why these attitudes? (See also Is. 33:32.)

3/How is the picture in Nahum different from Psalm 96?

What two seemingly contradictory streams of thought run through this section?

Comments
The justice of God leads directly to the judgment of God. The universe would be absurd if the God who created it and established its moral order did not pass a judgment upon it. That God eventually is going to judge the world is taken as axiomatic in Scripture. But it also follows logically from the fact of God's holiness. We have already seen how God's holiness leads to the establishing of his law which requires holiness of life on the part of his people. It must be expected, then, that at some time God will review how his law has been heeded.

God's judgment will mean two different things for people.

It will be a time of joyful reward for those made righteous by Jesus Christ. It will be a time of fearful wrath for those who have spurned the holy God.

Application

1/With what feelings do you face the prospect of God's judgment? (See Rom. 11:22.)

_____

_____

2/If God is the judge, how should you evaluate yourself and others (cf. Mt. 7:1; 1 Cor. 4:3-5)? Why?

_____

_____

_____

3/Note the commands of Psalm 96 which are given in light of God's coming to judge. How can you obey them?

_____

_____

_____

Further Study

1/Read "The Wrath of God" in *The Living God,* pages 64-66.

2/Study what Jesus says about judgment in John 5:19-29 and Matthew 25:31-46. How does the latter section relate to study 4 in this topic?

3/The doctrine of God's judgment is hateful to some and embarrassing to others. God's holiness and judgment may seem to contradict his love and mercy. How do you reconcile these attributes?

THE GOODNESS OF GOD

When we study the **goodness** of God we see God in compassionate relationship with his creation. By the "goodness of God" we refer specifically to those qualities of God by which he is beneficent toward his creatures. God's goodness is that characteristic of his nature by which he is motivated to do things which are good for us. That goodness is an attribute of God is one of the unique features of God's revelation of himself in the Bible. Apart from biblical revelation mankind has never conceived of a god who was good in the way Scripture shows the true God to be. The gods of men's imagination have sometimes been mighty, they have been creators, they have been lawgivers and stern judges. Men have ascribed to them several of the characteristics we have seen in the true God up to this point in our study. But they have not had the compassionate relationship with men and the world that the Bible declares God to have. Only through God's own revelation of himself do we learn about his mercy, grace, long-suffering, forgiveness, faithfulness and love.

study 1
the goodness of god

Exodus 33:12–34:10

Questions

1/About what is Moses concerned in his dialogue with God (33:13-18)?

2/For what does Moses specifically ask God?

3/When Moses asks God to show his glory, what does God say he will show him (33:19)?

4/When Moses receives the revelation God promised him, with what characteristics does God describe himself (34:6-7)?

L.I.F.E. College Library
1100 Glendale Blvd.
Los Angeles, Calif. 90026

5/In what specific ways does God promise to demonstrate his goodness?

_____

_____

_____

6/What does this experience show about the person to whom God will reveal himself?

_____

_____

Comments

We know the personal characteristics of someone only when he discloses them to us. When Moses asked God to show him his glory, God promised to make all his goodness pass before him and in this disclosure to show what his name really was. (Recall from Topic A, study 2, the Hebrew custom regarding one's name.) Moses had hitherto learned much about God but in this experience God took him into more intimate knowledge of himself than he had ever enjoyed. When God proclaimed his goodness to Moses he listed his attributes of mercy, grace, patience, love, forgiveness and faithfulness. These characteristics show what God really is like as the personal God who chooses to enter into compassionate relationship with his people. Our succeeding studies will explore each characteristic in more detail.

Application

1/How is Moses' relationship and response to God an example for you to follow?

_____

_____

2/Have you experienced the goodness of God in your life? If so, list some specific examples.

_____

_____

_____

_____

_____

_____

Further Study
See "The Goodness of God," chapter 16 in *The Knowledge of the Holy*.

study 2
the mercy of God

Psalm 103

Questions

1/List the characteristics and deeds of God for which he is worshipped in this psalm.

_____

_____

_____

_____

_____

_____

_____

_____

_____

2/Verses 8-18 concentrate on that attribute of God usually called *mercy*. Two English synonyms of mercy are used here: "pity" and "steadfast love." How is God's mercy described in the following verses:

verse 8:

verse 10:

verse 11:

verse 13:

verse 14:

verses 15-17:

3/What general condition for God's mercy is mentioned in verse 18? (See also Ps. 32:10.)

4/Define mercy.

Comments
The biblical doctrine of the mercy of God reveals him relating to his creation specifically like a compassionate father. Paul praises God as the "Father of mercies" (2 Cor. 1:3).

God's mercy motivates him, like a father, to deliver his children from both physical and spiritual distress (Ps. 6:1-4).

Scripture teaches four things about God's mercy. (1) It is free and undeserved. No human deed can earn it. Otherwise it would not be mercy (Tit. 3:5). (2) It is exercised sovereignly. By his own unaffected choice, God "has mercy upon whomever he will" (Rom. 9:18). (3) It is boundless. God's mercy is new every morning (Lam. 3:23) and is as great as the heavens are high above the earth. (4) It is unending. It is God's nature always to be merciful (Ps. 103:17).

Application

1/What consolation is there for you in the fact that God "remembers that we are dust"?

2/What should be your response to the mercy of God (v. 18)? (See also Prov. 28:13.)

3/Jesus said: "Be ye merciful, as your heavenly Father is merciful." How can you practice mercy today in relation to the people with whom you have contact?

Further Study

1/See "The Mercy of God," chapter 18 in *The Knowledge of the Holy.*

2/Study *mercy* in Lamentations 3:22-25; Deuteronomy 5:10; 1 Chronicles 16:34; Isaiah 55:7; Psalm 62:12.

3/How could some people be misled by God's mercy? (Compare Ps. 103:9 with 2 Pet. 2:3-9; see also Deut. 29:18-20.)

4/Tozer says the notion "that justice and judgment characterize the God of Israel, while mercy and grace belong to the Lord of the Church" is erroneous (*The Knowledge of the Holy,* p. 97). Have you heard of this notion? How can you show that it is erroneous?

topic d
THE GOODNESS OF GOD

study 3
the grace of god

Ephesians 2:1-10
Questions
1/How does Paul describe the condition of his readers before God made them alive?

_____

_____

_____

2/Verses 4-7 give at least three factors motivating God to exercise his grace. What are they? (Compare v. 7 with 1:6.)

_____

_____

_____

3/Explain the function of the word "for" at the beginning of verse 8.

_____

_____

4/What does Paul teach here about how one is saved? What is the opposite of grace?

Comments

The mercy and the grace of God are interrelated concepts and Scripture frequently includes them in the same breath (2 Chron. 30:9; Joel 2:13; Heb. 4:16). The distinction between them is not easily drawn, but it might be expressed epigrammatically in this way: *Mercy* is that quality by which God does *not* give to sinners what they *do* deserve (i.e., punishment: "It is of the Lord's mercy that we are not consumed"); *grace* is that quality by which God *does* give to sinners what they do *not* deserve (that is, salvation: "By grace you have been saved"). Thus, Scripture indicates that God has *mercy* to all (Ps. 145:9) but never is *grace* mentioned in any other connection than with those who are saved.

Grace is the unearned goodness of God extended to those who have no claim to it and who are by nature under a sentence of condemnation. In Scripture the grace of God is both (1) that quality by which God gives something to us and (2) the gift itself (Rom. 5:15). In the former case, "favor" is a good synonym. In the latter case, "energy" represents the idea underlying the word "grace." That is, because God has the quality of grace (favor) toward us, he infuses us with the grace (energy) to respond to him. That response is referred to as "faith." *By nature* we are enemies of God and not at all inclined to come to him; *by mercy* God does not visit upon us his wrath which our rebellion deserves; *by grace* God determines to change our nature so that we will come to him, and *by grace* he changes our nature so that *by faith* we respond to him.

Application

1/What does Paul teach here about good works in salvation?

_____

_____

About good works in the Christian life?

_____

_____

2/What should you do if you have experienced God's grace (v. 8; see also Heb. 4:14-16)?

_____

_____

_____

Further Study
1/See "The Grace of God," chapter 19 in *The Knowledge of the Holy.*
2/What does Exodus 33:19 teach about God's grace?
3/Using a concordance, look up every reference in Scripture which includes the words "grace," "gracious" and "favor" and determine for yourself a definition of the grace of God.
4/See *In Understanding Be Men,* pages 136-141.

topic d
THE GOODNESS OF GOD

study 4
the longsuffering of god

Nehemiah 9:6-37
Questions
1/Briefly summarize how this account establishes the point that God is "slow to anger."

_____

_____

_____

_____

2/What sins of the Jewish people are mentioned? Why did they act in these ways (vv. 25, 28)?

_____

_____

_____

_____

_____

3/In what ways did God respond to their *sins* (vv. 18-19, 27-28, 30-31, 37)? Why did God act in different ways at different times?

4/In what ways did God respond to their *repentance* (vv. 27-28)?

5/What was the reason for this historical review (vv. 32-37)?

Comments

This passage underscores the fullness of the goodness of God in his relation to Israel, and we can find here each of the elements of his goodness (see Topic D, study 1). Let us concentrate, however, on God's dealing with his people when they sin. Two responses of God to sin are shown. (1) God bears with sin and does not immediately sever his relations with his sinning people (v. 31). God is merciful and long-suffering. His good gifts to us are not results of our bargaining with him as if he does good for us as long as we do not sin. God freely gives out of his goodness and patiently bears with our sin. Scripture uses the descriptive phrase "slow to anger" (Nahum 1:3) to express God's longsuffering (patience).

But (2) when there is continued rebellion against God, expressed in no love for him and disobedience to his laws, then he no longer postpones judgment; he punishes the sinful people. The alternative to continued rebellion is repentance, which is expressed here as a return to God (see also 2 Chron. 5:36-39). Repentance is not primarily sorrow for sinfulness but the positive action of returning to God (Is. 55:7).

Application

1/What do you learn about sin in your life from this selection? How does it affect God's relationship with you? How does it affect your response to him?

2/What do you resolve now to do about sin in your life which you know about? List specific actions or attitudes.

3/How can you imitate the longsuffering of God in your relationships with others? (See Mt. 18:23-35.)

Further Study

1/How is the longsuffering of God expressed beyond the bounds of his own people, to the world at large (Acts 17:28-31; Rom. 3:25; 2 Pet. 3:8-9; Gen. 6:3)?

study 5
the forgiveness of god

Psalm 51
Questions
1/On what basis does David ask for forgiveness (vv. 1, 13)?

2/What does David say about sin (vv. 4-5)?

3/What is God's response to sin (v. 4) and to sacrifices (i.e., religious activities to make up for sin, v. 16)?

4/For what does David ask in verses 6-12? Why does David ask not only for forgiveness but for "a new and right spirit"?

_____ _____

_____

_____

_____

5/Refer back to Psalm 32:1-5. What happened when David did not acknowledge his sin? When he did?

_____

_____

Comments

"For thou, O Lord, art good and forgiving" (Ps. 86:5). In yesterday's study we saw two responses of God to sin: forbearance and punishment. Today we concentrate upon a third response: forgiveness. God bears with sin so that his people will confess their sin so that he can forgive and punishment will be unnecessary.

God forgives because his nature inclines him to do so. We can expect him to forgive (Jon. 4:2). But that forgiveness is experienced only by those who acknowledge their need for forgiveness (1 Jn. 1:5-10). David realized that it was his nature to sin (v. 5). We cannot avoid sinning. To sin is just the way we are, and without God's help we cannot do otherwise. If we are willing to acknowledge our sin, we receive God's forgiveness and cleansing. If we are not willing, then God's holiness manifests itself in judgment. Confession is not merely a religious activity in which we list our sins and then God must automatically excuse them. Psalm 51:16-19 puts the lie to that idea. Our confession _allows_ God to act; it does not force him to act. God forgives not out of obligation but because that is his way of acting. Therefore, without anxiety, we can tell God we know we have sinned and receive his forgiveness.

Application
1/"The goodness of God leads you to repentance" (Rom. 2:4). Confess your sins to God in grateful response to his goodness and enjoy his forgiveness.

2/What was David's responsibility after receiving forgiveness (vv. 13-15)? What is yours?

_____

_____

_____

3/How can you imitate the forgiveness of God? What does Jesus teach about forgiving others (Mt. 6:12, 14-15)?

_____

_____

_____

Further Study
1/David's confession here follows his blatant sins of adultery and murder. Read the story of his actions in 2 Samuel 11:1-27, and the account of the way God caused him to face up to his sin, 2 Samuel 12:1-14. What consequences of David's sin does Nathan list (2 Sam. 12:7-14)? See how these occurred (2 Sam. 12:15-23; 15:1-10; 16:20-23). God forgave David's sin, but the consequences followed nonetheless. What does this show about the way God deals with sin and about the nature of forgiveness?

study 6
the faithfulness of god

Deuteronomy 7:6-12
Jeremiah 30:22—31:20

Questions

1/For what two reasons did God save the Israelites from their bondage in Egypt?

2/How does God respond to those who love him? To those who hate him? Why does he respond in these ways?

3/When Jeremiah wrote, over 600 years after Moses spoke the words in Deuteronomy, God's people were languishing in exile where God had sent them as punishment. What consolation does Jeremiah give to the suffering people?

4/What determined God's way of dealing with his people (Jer. 31:3; see also Ps. 119:75)?

5/At this point in time, what had their experiences taught the Israelites about God (Jer. 31:17-20)?

Comments

"If we are faithless, he remains faithful—for he cannot deny himself" (2 Tim. 2:13). God's goodness is everlasting because he is changeless. Since it is his nature to be "merciful and gracious, slow to anger and abounding in steadfast love," he will always be like this toward his people. This is what the people of Israel learned vividly through the history of their relationship with their God. Even when they disobeyed God, even when he had to punish them, he remained faithful to his covenant promises to them because he had taken them as his children.

Because God is faithful he demonstrates his goodness. He keeps his promises (Ps. 89:33-35). He preserves his people (1 Pet. 4:19). He keeps them as his own (Jn. 10:28). He answers their prayers (Ps. 143:1). He protects them from evil (1 Cor. 10:13, 2 Thess. 3:3). He punishes to correct them (Ps. 119:75). He receives them back (1 Sam. 12:20-22) and forgives their sin (1 Jn. 1:9). All of this because God is faithful.

Application

1/What comfort do you get for your own life from the fact of God's faithfulness?

2/How have you experienced the faithfulness of God as the Israelites did?

_____

_____

_____

3/How can you be faithful to God?

_____

_____

4/How can you reflect the faithfulness of God in your life (for example, in your duties, your personal relationships)?

_____

_____

_____

Further Study

1/See "The Faithfulness of God" in _The Living God,_ pages 88-92.

2/Worship God for those things about himself which he has shown you this week. Worship is the highest act to which God calls his people. Worship is concentrating the mind upon God himself. (1) It consists in taking account of his attributes. We can do this by listing and meditating upon all the attributes of God that occur to us. It is often helpful to use the psalms to bring the qualities of God to our minds. (2) It consists in taking account of what God has done, as evidences of what he is like. Thus, by reviewing what God did in history and what he is doing in our lives, we are reminded of what he is like.

THE LOVE OF GOD

"God so loved the world that he gave his only Son, that whoever believes in him should not perish but have eternal life." This statement is probably the most widely known verse of Scripture. And rightly so. For the truth that God put his love into action for the benefit of sinful men, at the cost of his own beloved Son, is the greatest fact of history. Scripture bears witness on almost every page that the God of the universe is a God of love. The holy, almighty God desires to enter into direct, intimate, personal relationship with his creatures, for love seeks out and communicates with its object.

In the studies on the topic of God's love, after first exploring one New Testament section that shows love as a fundamental characteristic of God's nature, we shall concentrate on one book of the Old Testament which vividly portrays God's love. The book of Hosea is a parable of God's love in which God uses the prophet's marriage to illustrate the way God loves his own people. We shall understand love better by seeing it in action than by treating it only as a subject of intellectual discourse.

study 1
"god is love"

1 John 4:7-21

Questions

1/List what John says about what God is like and what he has done.

_____

_____

_____

_____

_____

_____

_____

_____

2/List what John says about love.

_____

_____

L.I.F.E. College Library
1100 Glendale Blvd.
Los Angeles, Calif. 90026

_____

_____

_____

_____

_____

_____

3/What is the difference between saying "God is love" and "God loves"?

_____

_____

_____

4/To what does John point as evidence that God is love? State precisely how this is an evidence of God's love.

_____

_____

_____

5/What is the connection between God's love for us, our love for him and our love for others?

_____

_____

Comments

John asserts the truth that God is love in order to support his injunction to believers to love others. John repeats the command on which Jesus placed particular emphasis, that the greatest duty God has laid upon us is to love him and to love one another (Mt. 22:36-40; Jn. 13:34). On first sight it might appear strange that God *commands* us to love. Is it possible to love in obedience to a command? Is not love an emotion which lies beyond the reach of a command?

John shows that the power to obey this requirement derives from God's nature. When he says "God is love," John emphasizes that love characterizes God's very essence and being. True love flows out of God's nature, for "love is of God." Those who participate in the divine nature in Christ (2 Pet. 1:4) have a divine energy within themselves. So they have the power to love by releasing that energy, allowing it to express itself in relation to others. Love is a matter of the will. We can obey God's command to love because God performs a special act of grace within us (Deut. 30:6). Conversely, if we love we give evidence that God has touched our lives. "He who loves is born of God and knows God."

Application

1/What three reasons does John give for loving others? Differentiate among these reasons and show how each is reasonable.

2/What answer does John provide for the person who objects, "I just cannot love"?

3/In what *specific* areas of your life do you need to practice more love?

Further Study

1/John Stott writes: "For the loveless Christian to profess to know God and to have been born of God is like claiming to be intimate with a foreigner whose language we cannot speak, or to have been born of parents whom we do not in any way resemble" (*The Epistles of John,* London: Tyndale, 1964, p. 161). What does today's Scripture say that supports and explains this statement?

2/From the following verses, write a description of the kind of love which God shows: Deuteronomy 7:7-10; Jeremiah 31:3; Matthew 5:44-45; Romans 5:7-8; John 3:16.

3/Read "The Love of God," chapter 20 in *The Knowledge of the Holy.*

4/See the studies on love in *Grow Your Christian Life,* pages 3-10.

study 2
a parable of god's love: hosea's marriage

Hosea 1 and 3

Questions

1/Write a brief synopsis of the story of Hosea's marriage.

_____

_____

_____

2/What is the significance of the names Hosea gave to his children?*

_____

_____

_____

3/What is the future to be for Israel (1:4-5, 10-11; 3:4-5)?

_____

_____

_____

_____

4/What was Hosea like? Think of the sorrow he must have experienced.

_____

_____

5/How is God's love illustrated in this section?

_____

_____

Comments

God communicated his messages to the Jews through his chosen mouthpieces, the prophets. They were not mechanical loudspeakers, however. They were normal human beings who lived much like the rest of their society, with their own personal sorrows and joys. But they were especially aware of God. The prophets differed from each other in personality and experiences, and God used these differences to his advantage in getting through to the people.

It would appear that Hosea was a tender man, very much aware of the love and mercy of God, and thus Hosea was especially appropriate for God to use in communicating the fact of his love for his people. Hosea's experiences in his life were much like the history of God's relationship with Israel. Hosea's wife was unfaithful to him as Israel was unfaithful to God. But Hosea still loved his wife as God steadfastly loved Israel. It was because of these similarities that God could choose to convey a special message about his love through Hosea. God's love for Israel was like a husband's love for his wife.

Application

1/God occasionally allows unhappy events to come into our lives, as he did into Hosea's. What should be our attitude toward these difficulties? (See Job 1:21; 2 Cor. 1:3-4; 1 Pet. 4:16.)

Further Study

1/Read "The Love of God" in *The Living God,* pages 85-92.

2/Learn more about the cultural and historical setting of Hosea and the general message of the book by consulting *The New Bible Commentary* and "Hosea" in *The New Bible Dictionary.*

3/There is a legitimate question of interpretation of the story of Hosea's marriage: Was it historical fact, a vision or an allegory? Definite conclusion is difficult. God could have used an experience within Hosea's imagination in order to communicate his message about love. But it seems more likely that the story is historical. What do you think?

*notes: v. 4 "Jezreel": a valley in Israel where Jehu killed the royal family of Ahab and established his own revolutionary government (2 Kings 9 and 10).

v. 6 "Not pitied," in Hebrew, *lo-ruhamah,* means "unloved." Perhaps this child was not Hosea's; perhaps he was unsure whether she was his.

v. 9 "Not my people," in Hebrew, *lo-ammi,* means "not mine." This child was certainly not Hosea's.

study 3
god the bridegroom

Hosea 2

Questions

1/What is the significance in the reversal of the children's names?

2/This chapter is an explanation of the parabolic message in Hosea's marriage. God takes the place of Hosea and Israel takes the place of his wife. What misunderstandings does the mother have (vv. 2-13)?

3/What evils (punishment) does God forecast for Israel?

What two responses will Israel have (v. 7)?

4/What does this chapter show about the purpose of punishment?

5/How is verse 14 a picture of intense love? (Compare vv. 16, 19-20.)

What is the logical force of "therefore" in verse 14?

6/What does God promise to Israel?

Comments
God's relationship to the Jews is frequently compared to that of a husband and wife: The Jews' frequent forgetting of God was compared to adultery or prostitution (see Hos. 9:1). The "wife" had been born in Egyptian bondage—naked and helpless as a baby; courtship was the time of deliverance out of this bondage (the Exodus); the marriage was the covenant

God made with Israel at Mount Sinai (Ex. 24:7-8). God gave his "wife" a pleasant place to live ("a land flowing with milk and honey") but she misunderstood and forsook the benevolences of her "husband" (see Ezek. 16:6-43). The Old Testament writers frequently associated national apostasy with prostitution—referring to "playing the harlot after strange gods" (Deut. 31:16). But even though unfaithful, the "wife" was still loved by her "husband" (Hos. 3:1), and he intended to woo her back to his love (2:14). In this God shows that his love is enduring (see Is. 49:14-16).

Application
1/In what ways do verses 19 and 20 describe your relationship with God? In what ways is your relationship to God lacking in these characteristics?

2/What comfort do you get from this section for a time when you have been (or will be) unfaithful to God?

3/How does James 4:4-5 underscore an application of this section?

Further Study
1/In the New Testament, Christians are pictured as being the "wife" of Christ. It is helpful to us that God compared his relationship with his people to marriage,

since we can learn abou. our relationship to God by examining marriage, and we can learn how married people should behave toward each other by examining God's relationship to his people (see Eph. 5:23, 25). What do you learn from Hosea 2 about proper conduct in marriage?

2/See how Paul (Rom. 9:22-26) and Peter (1 Pet. 2:9-10) use the message of Hosea in applying it to Gentile Christians.

3/Read "Adultery and Apostasy" in *The Church at the End of the 20th Century* by Francis A. Schaeffer (IVP), pages 113-29.

study 4
israel's sin

Hosea 4:1-14

Questions

1/List all the sins for which the Lord finds fault with Israel (vv. 1-4).

_____

_____

_____

_____

2/What are the results of their sins? (See Joel 1:4; Amos 7:1-6.)

_____

_____

3/What fault does God find with the religious leaders (vv. 6-10)?

_____

_____

_____

4/Verses 11-14 condemn false religion. What sins are committed?

Comments
The adultery of Israel consisted in unfaithfulness in two areas: social justice and religious worship.

(1) Israel failed to exercise truth and goodness in society; she violated God's laws without fear; there was, in sum, no love of the good. But God is a God of holiness, justice and goodness, as we have seen in earlier studies. Any rejection of these values by those who claim to be his people is unfaithfulness to God.

(2) Israel practiced pagan and idolatrous religion which grew out of the error of thinking that God was different than he really is (v. 6a). This manifested itself in several wrong practices: (a) sacrifices that were misused (v. 8); (b) erroneous methods for finding God's will (v. 12); (c) religious observances that were forbidden by God (v. 13—tops of mountains were common places of pagan worship; see Deut. 12:2-5) including religious prostitution, a common pagan practice. But God's requirement is "goodness, not sacrifice, and the knowledge of God more than burnt offerings" (Hos. 6:6).

Application
1/What suggestions do you derive from this study about how you can practice faithfulness to God?

_____

_____

_____

_____

2/One of the principal reasons for Israel's sinfulness was lack of true knowledge of God (vv. 1, 6). Consider Hosea 6:6. How can you continue to know God? Outline several steps you might take.

_____

_____

_____

_____

Pray about implementing this plan.

3/What instruction and warning can be drawn from this section for those who are called by God to positions of Christian leadership (especially vv. 6-9)?

_____

_____

_____

4/What parallels are there between Hosea's time and ours?

_____

_____

_____

Further Study

1/Compare this study (especially Hos. 4:1) with study 4 in Topic C.

2/This section is very critical of religious practices. But surely the conclusion to be drawn from this is not that all religious practices should be rejected. How does true knowledge of God affect religious practices?

study 5
god's punishment

Hosea 11:1-9
Hebrews 12:5-13

Questions

1/How has Hosea changed the metaphor by which God's love is depicted?

_____

2/How is God's love for his people described (vv. 1, 3-4, 8)?

_____

_____

_____

_____

3/How did the people repay the Lord for his love?

_____

_____

4/What attributes of God are mentioned or alluded to here?

_____

_____

_____

_____

5/What is taught about God's relationship to his people when they forget him (vv. 5-9)? How does this show the quality in God of "justice tempered with mercy"?

_____

_____

_____

6/In Hebrews 12:5-13, what is taught about God as the Father and his people as his children?

_____

_____

Why does God punish his children (vv. 6, 10-11)?

_____

_____

_____

7/What assurance does God's punishment give (vv. 7-8)?

_____

_____

Comments
God's love is like that of a father for his children as well as like that of a husband for his wife. In this metaphor the

tenderness of God's love is especially emphasized. God showed careful concern for his son, Israel. He brought him up in love and gentleness. But his son did not recognize all that God did for him and wandered away from God, almost as if he were "bent on backsliding," as if he had no other design but to disobey. God would have been quite justified in utterly destroying Israel for its sinfulness. But God's justice is tempered by his love, and he determines to punish not solely in satisfaction of justice but with an aim to correction. God punishes those he has chosen as his own children in order to correct their wrongs and make them partakers of his holiness so that they will imitate the one they call Father (1 Pet. 1:15-17).

Application
1/What does Hosea 11:9 teach you about God's punishment when you sin? How does this affect your attitude toward God?

2/How should you respond if God punishes you (Heb. 12:12-13)?

3/Does it sometimes seem that you, too, are "bent on turning away" from God? How can you expect God to deal with this?

Further Study

1/What can be learned from this study about the raising of children?

2/Compare Hosea 11:1 with Exodus 4:22-23. How is verse 1 used in Matthew 2:15? What do you make of this?

study 6
response to god's love

Hosea 14

Questions

1/List the steps and evidences of repentance given in this chapter.

2/What three sins of Israel are mentioned in verse 3?

3/List what God will do for Israel in response to repentance.

How does this response correspond to the promise God gave in 2 Chronicles 7:13-22?

4/How is God's love described in verse 4? What does this mean?

Comments
We cannot experience the greatness of God's love personally without first returning to God in a whole-hearted repentance which is accompanied with all appropriate external actions. The return to God is the essence of conversion ("conversion" means "turning around"). We have had occasion in this series to note God's rejection of sacrifice and worship sometimes because his desire is for outward justice and inward righteousness before external ritual.

Verse 2 in this chapter is his call for the sacrifice which he finds acceptable: praise, "the fruit of our lips." As the psalmist phrased it: "The sacrifice acceptable to God is a broken spirit; a broken and contrite heart, O God, thou wilt not despise" (Ps. 51:17).

Verse 4 emphasizes the great biblical fact that, although one must repent and come to God, God's love for him is absolutely unmerited: "I will love them *freely.*" And even the return to God is the result of his work in the returner: "I will heal their faithlessness" (recall Topic D, study 3).

Application
1/What steps of repentance do you need to take in response to God's love?

2/In what areas do you need wisdom, discernment and up-rightness in your life (v. 9)?

_____

_____

_____

3/What have you learned this week about God's love?

_____

_____

Thank him for what you should thank him for; praise him for what you should praise him for.

Epilogue
Verse 9 is the conclusion for the entire book of Hosea. "These things" refers to all of the message of Hosea's prophecy. Hosea emphasized that the chief fault of the people was their lack of knowledge of God. Only with correct understanding of God's nature and God's message will life be correctly lived. Thus Paul said that Scripture is given to us "for teaching, for reproof, for correction, for instruction in right living, that the man of God may be complete."

Verse 9 is also a fitting conclusion for our entire series, for we have been studying to become wise in order that we may understand "these things" about God, and discerning so that we may know them, and we trust that we shall be more ready to follow the ways of the Lord, that is, his glory, his very nature.

for further study from InterVarsity Press

KNOWING GOD
J. I. Packer writes about the nature of God in a profound and deeply moving way. John Stott says of this book, ". . . the truth he handles fires the heart. At least it fired mine, and compelled me to turn aside to worship and to pray." 867-X cloth $5.95

GETTING TO KNOW JESUS
Paul Steeves supplies daily studies in the same format as the present volume, exploring what Scripture tells us about Jesus' deity, lordship, love, death and resurrection. 663-4 $1.50

GROW YOUR CHRISTIAN LIFE
Twelve weeks of Bible studies direct personal or group exploration of such topics as new life in Christ, faith and doubt, knowing God's will, marriage and Christian fellowship. Designed for daily 25-minute studies. 661-8 $1.50

LEARNING TO BE A MAN
LEARNING TO BE A WOMAN
Kenneth and Floy Smith, in these companion volumes, show what it is to become a man and a woman. These study guides point you—an individual, a couple, a group—to God and to the Bible. They don't make the learning easy, but they certainly make it possible. And what you learn is yours to keep. *Learning to Be a Man* 692-8 $1.50; *Learning to Be a Woman* 693-6 $1.50

THE LIVING GOD
R. T. France takes the approach of biblical theology and conveys the excitement of learning who God has revealed himself to be. 697-9 $1.50

IN UNDERSTANDING BE MEN
T. C. Hammond outlines major Christian doctrines, presents divergent views and their bases, then lists pertinent Scripture passages. 705-3 $1.95

L.I.F.E. College Library
1100 Glendale Blvd.
Los Angeles, Calif. 90026